GREEN TEA And DONUTS

6 Simple Steps for
Living Your Best Life

DR. CARLENE RANDOLPH

Green Tea and Donuts

6 Simple Ways to Live Your Best Life

© 2018 Carlene Randolph

All Rights Reserved. No portion of this publication may be reproduced, stored in any electronic system, or transmitted in any form or by any means (electronic, mechanical, photocopy, recording or otherwise) without written permission from the publisher. Mild quotations may be used for literary reviews.

Published in Dallas, Georgia, by SBG Media Group and Publishing™.

ISBN 978-1-7327340-2-9

Library of Congress Control Number 2018958555

Available in electronic book also.

SBG Media Group and Publishing™

Dallas, GA

www.thescatterbrainedgenius.com/publishing

Green Tea and Donuts

6 Simple Ways to Live Your Best Life

DEDICATION

There are those who mark their own paths in life and those that have a special gift in showing others the way as they succeed. These highly motivated women have one thing in common, they inspire others to become all that they can be and more.

This is a book for those women who want to level up while becoming and inspiration for others that may come behind them.

FOREWORD

Green Tea and Donuts is much needed concept of women empowerment and growth. As a coach myself I see how valuable it is to provide encouragement and guidance to women who seek to change their lives. Coach Cai does that with kindness and grace in this book. I love the personable way that it's written as if written by a close, caring friend providing actionable tools to succeed in all areas of personal growth!

Obianuju "Nikki" Anarado, CPC, PMP
Dating Preparation Coach,
Prepare to be Pursued

PREFACE

When I discovered that there were specific steps to take to reach my "live my best life" I was mortified that it had taken so many years. These steps were just what I needed since life had been so chaotic and fraught why so many stops and starting all over again. This was hardly an academic pursuit and honestly, I found that my very own journaling over the years gave me the right lessons, per se, to write this book. As I reviewed the many pages of the numerous journals I laughed, I cried, I found the path and inspiring and motivating as I remembered. Apparently, I found enjoyment in recognizing that there were in fact powerful lessons from the good, bad and horrendous events in my life.

My discovery of the six steps completely changed my view of how I would achieve future endeavors and discovering how I would restore what I believed was stolen from me by others not pouring what they learned about the road to success into me as I travelled my journey. These steps are simplistic yet powerful action-oriented solutions that I have shared with friends and clients over the years. The value that such actions bring into the lives of others is immeasurable and likely will be sustainable practices for years to come. I have shared these ideas and actions with many women who were embarking on huge life changes. Those individuals have asked me to share the message with their friends and so on. The idea of Green Tea and Donuts started to spread.

It was at this point that I decided to be my very own test dummy. It would not be right not to. I practiced every step wholly and it is the only reason I am who I have become today because of practicing these steps.

I do not have a publicist and no national press coverage and still the concept will spread because it resonates for many women because at the core we love and care about others. It is that sisterhood that will give life to Green Tea and Donuts spreading through the workshops I give and in community service activities. It will spread inherently because it a very optimistic and human---those who believe in it and who give themselves permission to live it, they will share it far and wide.

Carlene (Coach Cai) Randolph

ACKNOWLEDGEMENTS

There are far too many people to say thank you to however, with a heartfelt thanks to a few very significant people: To Mary Randolph, my mom and mentor, your spirit and enthusiasm (sometimes the lack of) makes me giggle to think you encourage me all the same to write this book. To Jay Kevin Blake, often my "Doubting Thomas" pushed me to prove my points and therefore, pushed me to stand alone and be strong enough to find my way. To Amanda Porter, and Cierstan Randolph, my daughters, I love you to the moon and beyond, it has always been you that said you believed in me when I waivered in my personal feelings. Thanks to Mona Kalsi, Maria Donner and Pinky Singh, my sister-friends, you always manage to give wise counsel beyond your years.

INTRODUCTION

Over the years, I have always considered myself like my mother in many ways. Heck: I looked and walked like her! At times, I even sounded just like my mom when I attempted to sing. Don't tell her I said this, but she could never carry a note—and neither could I. In many ways, I thought that I should shoulder the same responsibilities she carried. I often heard her say, "Women are expected to carry the weight of the world, while men made children and paid the bills." As I matured, I understood what she believed to be the truth. My dad would take the back seat to raising his daughter because he believed that only mom could impart what it meant to be "a woman in this man's world." There began my journey of finding me.

Ladies, in retrospect, many of us are taught to follow the rules—those tight constraints that made life more difficult than it had to be. In generations before mine, some women believed that if they followed those rules of engagement, they would find happiness and some form of success. Looking back on the many conversations I had with my mother and grandmother, once in a while, one of them would say, "I could have been…" or "I should have done…" I wonder: If they had those opportunities, what would their lives have looked like? I, too, struggled to follow those societal rules, only to find there were delicious, little donuts that intrigued me enough to divert me off of "Happiness and Success Road."

For example, I partied in college and had children. I dropped out of college, dated jocks and music industry entertainers, and the list goes on and on. My parents were devastated because I did not follow the rules. Still, I was also graced with the greatest opportunities in my career development as I learned the ropes from many of those who crossed my path. I learned to strategically plan both long- and short-term goals, negotiate contracts, and generate income at the drop of a hat. I was never afraid to experiment with challenging roles in the corporate world. I recognized I had an eye for identifying talented people and excelled at mentoring and coaching them to their successes. Over the years, I used those talents—along with the positive and harsh lessons to start businesses and lead changes in large organizations—to lead people through change and build relationships.

Today, my mother often tells our family and her friends, "She could shake up soda, and she'd expect the explosion to be golden nuggets." I am more than my mother's daughter: I am (in my own right) a force to be reckoned with. I marked my own pathways to successes, and my happiness comes from within. I know that the rules were my "green tea," and my freedom to talk away from those rules were my "donuts." I learned that I could have both, as I nod to the not-so-distant past and blaze a trail to redesign, rediscover, and reignite my passion and purpose as often as necessary.

Love and Light,

Coach Cai

TABLE OF CONTENTS

DEDICATION	iv
FOREWORD	v
PREFACE	vi
ACKNOWLEGEMENTS	viii
INTRODUCTION	ix

CHAPTER ONE	REDISCOVERING YOU	13
CHAPTER TWO	REDESIGNING YOU	26
CHPATER THREE	REIGNITING YOUR PASSION AND PURPOSE	48
CHAPTER FOUR	REACTIVATING INNER CONFIDENCE	61
CHAPTER FIVE	RETHINKING YOUR SUCCESS NETWORK	75
CHAPTER SIX	READY? SET! RELEASE! GEARING TO BE SUCCESSFUL	99

Chapter One

REDISCOVERING YOU

Mindset Matters
&
Failure
is a Fiction Novel

In an article titled *The Effort Effect* that is published on Stanford University's website, the author wrote about a popular soccer team called "The Blackburn Rovers." The Blackburn Rovers play in one of the most glamorous soccer leagues in the world: The English Premiership. As expected, the team has a training academy that is ranked among the top three in England, but there was a problem: Even though the players were all talented and very promising, they were failing to reach their potential. Even though the club's motto is "Skill and hard work," the players disliked training. The Performance Director suspected the source of the problem: There is a popular belief in the soccer community that great players are born—not made. That is to say: Practice doesn't make you great. If you are great, it is because you have it in you. If you are not, it is because you don't. That means if you have that mindset, why practice? What is the point?

For a very long time in the history of the world, women have always taken the back seat when it comes to issues that relate to and directly affect their lives. Across many cultures and geographical areas, many women have been raised with certain devastating mindsets. Many women are told that no matter what they do and how hard they study, they would never reach the top because "women just don't reach the top." These same women have been told that women are not smart enough to get doctoral degrees—except for the few exceptional ones. They have been told that they can't take up certain jobs because they are women. They have been told that having a great family and top career positions are mutually-exclusive events. They have been told they are not "that smart" because their gender is not predisposed to intelligence. Ladies, we can all see the results of those mindsets for ourselves today. Few women occupy important positions in society, fewer women fight for what they believe in, and even fewer women ever reach the top of their game and reach the pinnacle of their potentials.

According to Carol Dweck, a foremost psychologist, there are two types of mindsets: the fixed mindset and the growth mindset. When you have a fixed mindset, you believe that your skills are set in stone. You believe you have a certain level of intelligence that you cannot go beyond and believe that your strengths are set. You believe that you can't be better at math. You believe that you can't get a college degree because you just don't have the smarts for it. You believe that you have a fixed personality that can't be changed. You believe that you have a fixed moral character. For instance, you believe you are good with science but can never learn how to draw or play a musical instrument. You believe that it is just not for you. You believe you can't be a CEO because you have young children.

In reverse, people who have a growth mindset believe they can develop their skills and strengths through continuous efforts, even if it means it will stretch them. They don't let the fact that they struggled with high school math prevent them from getting a degree in the sciences, even if it means they would have to do math over and over again.

According to an article in *Psychology Today*, "When challenges occur, women with fixed mindsets typically play it safe and avoid risks too far outside of their comfort zones. As a result, talented women don't volunteer to lead committees, step up for important projects at work, or set goals that are challenging enough. Therefore, women aren't on the forefront of a manager's mind when it comes time for raises, promotions, and accolades."

When Dweck started her research, she pondered the question: What happens when you give children difficult problems to solve? She found that some see it as a challenge and an opportunity to learn more, while others see it as an impossible situation and that their intelligence is being subjected to judgment and scrutiny. She found that children who see tasks as learning opportunities have the growth mindset because they could learn and develop the skills they need to solve the problem. The second group of children have fixed mindsets. They have the belief that there was nothing they could do to tackle a problem that is outside of their knowledge and problem-solving abilities.

Does mindset matter that much? You bet it does!

Your mindset plays a huge role in how you cope with the challenges in your life. In school, at work, and in relationships with others, a growth mindset can contribute to greater achievement and increased effort. When going through a challenging time, such as getting a new job, people with growth mindsets show greater resilience. They are more likely to push on in the face of setbacks, while those with fixed mindsets are likely to give up easily. People with fixed mindsets often yearn for approval. They see every situation as a call for confirmation of their intelligence, personality, or character. They evaluate their abilities with doubts in their minds:

- Will I succeed?
- Will I fail?
- Will I be accepted?
- What will be their impression of me if this doesn't go well?
- What if I lose?

On the other hand, people with growth mindsets have a burning hunger for learning. They have a desire to work hard and discover new things. They want to tackle challenges and grow. When people with a growth mindset try something, and it doesn't work out, they do not see it as a failure or disappointment. Instead, they see it as an opportunity to learn—an opportunity that can lead to growth and positive change.

Having a growth mindset doesn't always mean you believe that anyone can become whatever they desire to become through education and effort. No; not everyone can become an Einstein or Picasso. But everyone can become their own Einstein or Picasso. Everyone can live up to their highest potential. What that potential is, no one knows. No one knows how far a person can go if they set their mind to it. There really is no ceiling to improvement. If you have the growth mindset, you will believe that the effort and learning are worth all the trouble and toiling.

Can a mindset be changed? Definitely yes!

It all begins with you. You need to start looking beyond past failures and into the future to see what you can become. Your life is what you make it. It is your creation. Even though at this stage in your life, many people have helped influence your mindset—from parents to teachers, peers, and even society in general—all of this can be changed. You have all it takes to make your life incredible and successful. Your life is not something that just happened to you. Your life is your creation, and you have all it takes to make it very incredible and be what you want it to be. If you think that your life is out of control, it is because you have chosen not to be in control. You have abandoned your position as its architect. You are going to experience improvement in your life when you realize that you play the biggest role in what happens to you.

The change in mindset may not happen straight away. It most likely will not happen instantly, but if you make small, incremental changes in your life, it is only a matter of time before you start to see that you are a completely changed human being. The best place to start is to begin with the mindset of commitment and ownership of an end-result before you start out doing something. You must stop blaming your problems and failures—whether big or small—on the people around you. You need to stop giving excuses, such as, "It was a circumstance beyond my control," as the reason for your own actions, decisions, choices, and inactions. You must maintain accountability for your actions and adopt a mindset of taking on more responsibility for your life.

It was Bob Moawad who said, "The best day of your life is the one on which you decide that your life is your own. No apologies or excuses. No one to lean on, rely on, or blame. The gift is yours—it is an amazing journey—and you alone are responsible for the quality of it. This is the day that your life truly begins."

The issue with some of us is that we stop making attempts in life because we are scared that things will not be perfect. But if you are always waiting for the perfect outcome, every goal in your life will pass you by. What is important is to make plans and move on. If you can't get your mind off the thought that things may not work well, then instead, you can take some time thinking up a plan of action to take when things don't go as you have planned. They key thing is to take action. A lifetime spent making mistakes takes you closer to goals and is more honorable than one speculating and never taking action.

You may have planned to have your own business, gotten a degree, and started a family by the time you are 30 years old, but it looks like the right man is not coming along and you can't even get the funds needed to start your business at this time. For some people, the next line of action is to quit the whole plan and assume the universe and everyone in it is against them, instead of seeing the current situation as a challenge that happens in life. We all know life is not perfect, but it is our reaction to life's circumstances that make the difference. Your plans to get the funding you need for that business next year may not work out as expected, but quitting your dream of becoming an entrepreneur because you cannot get the funds you seek right now is a recipe for a failure of a lifetime. Don't stop trying. If plans aren't working out, seek them out and adapt them when necessary. We can't predict life's events with 100% accuracy, but that is okay. What we should be able to do is be ready for a change. This is what makes life so fun and interesting! In the light of uncertainty, there is room for a host of possibilities.

For many of the things we will set out to achieve in our lives, getting started will be the most difficult thing to do. Afterward, things will become pretty much normal. Most big endeavors start out hard. The beginning sucks. Think about the construction of a building. Preparing the foundation is often harder than putting things together above ground. In fact, anyone in construction will tell you that breaking the ground is the hard part. Getting started is the hard part. Getting the design, approvals, and funding are the parts that give the most headaches. As soon as that is out of the way, the remainder is not that difficult. Sometimes, however, even though there is a plan for construction, some unforeseen circumstances happen. Cost of raw materials could rise, weather could change, etc., and all of this could pose a threat to the project. Does that mean the project should stop? No! The goal of any builder or construction engineer is to see that the project reaches completion, despite the challenges. It is what builds a reputation and gets commendation. No one wants to hire a quitter to oversee their projects. This same concept applies to life.

You don't have to be great to start anything that you care about; however, the best time to start is now if you want to experience greatness in your life. The decision to start is the biggest and most important step you can ever take. You want to author a book? Start writing your thoughts down now. You want to get a job? Start preparing for the interview now. You need funding for your business? Start practicing your pitch now. Stammering now is okay. It is okay not to know what to say. It is also okay to fail at it a few times. What is not okay is to stop. Don't let failure get the best of you. Take all the chances you can. That's how you grow. The pain from the process will feed your courage.

People with fixed mindsets quit the moment they experience that first disappointment. They don't realize it is all a test that they have to fight their way through. This is what matters. People with growth mindsets stick around and keep pushing until they figure it out and get it. It is like being a parent. Many women want to be parents—you know...have a baby with cute eyes and adorable face. But good parenting is not the easiest of things. It may be very difficult with your first child, but as you birth more children, you settle into it. Parenting becomes a part of you. You may not even like it, but you do become better at it.

The biggest impediment to creativity and success is impatience; the desire to hasten things up and make a quick splash. If you want to be the best at anything, you need to overcome the initial resistance and keep on moving and practicing. When you start to see and believe that you can do no wrong, then you lose the edge that keeps you from progress and are open to new opportunities for growth.

Growth and continuous improvement are what matter. The world rewards people who get things done, not people who are reaching for perfection. When you are stuck in a rut, allow yourself the opportunity to wonder about what is possible and make the little moves in that direction. You don't need to make giant leaps, just little incremental moves. Following through and finishing things are very important tasks that you can teach yourself.

Screwing up is part of the process. Don't beat yourself up for making a mistake or wrong choice: You will only end

Many of us were born into a plan. We were given our lives to live. We were told to look at Chad, Meredith, Dr. Charles, and the lovely couple next door. For many of us, it started at childhood. Flip a switch, and the light will come on. Go to school, and your life is set. The people who cared for us wanted the best for us and created templates for us to work with. They do this with the best intentions, based on their personal experiences and those of the people they know. If you see a parent who fights tooth-and-nail for their children to go to college, it is because they have seen or experienced firsthand what a lack of a college degree can do to one's life economically or mentally. So, as soon as they start having children, they start creating a plan and template for them to follow. Now, this in itself is not a bad thing, as having children without a plan is worse; however, the danger of being born into a plan is that your life is handed to you with the least resistance by the planner. So, instead of living the life the way you want, you live it the way you have been given, and because all you have ever done is based on someone else's plan, your life grinds to a halt when something doesn't go according to the plan.

You study a course in college because you were told it would give you financial security, but you don't like it or care about it. You do it because the stakeholders want you to do it. You are not ready to get married yet, but the stakeholders keep reminding you that you are in your 30s and don't have much time left, so you register with any dating app you can find and go out on dates with anyone you can find. At the end of the day, you come home feeling empty, wondering how you got to where you are. The answer is not difficult: You are yet to find you.

You might encounter experiences in your life when you feel like what you're doing is just not enough. You might feel as if you're not contributing enough. However, you have to realize that sometimes, even doing enough or giving more might not be enough.

My conscience was filled, and I knew I was birthing a phenomenal project, yet I still needed to ignite my heart for its sake. Yes, I needed to shift and move on to fulfilling my dream of writing and inspiring others while doing so. Hence, I started a blog which today has become a successful project. The dream expanded and now, I'm on social media platforms hosting workshops and even speaking at events across the country. Wow! Because I wanted to live in my purpose, I'm filled with joy, happiness, and peace.

If you feel unhappy with the way your life is going and you feel as if you're not productive enough, it is time to rethink and reassess yourself.

Here is what you need to do: You need to pause and interrupt that pattern of behavior. Ask yourself the following questions, as the answers to them will serve as the roadmap to designing for yourself the life that will give you the fulfillment you need.

- What do I want?
  I know. This is a tough question for many of us, but really: What do you really want? What do you want your life to look like? What do you want to be

doing every day? Do you want to leave a legacy? Do you even care about it? Do you want to be really good at something that you will be the go-to person for? Do you even want to have children? The answers to these questions are important, but...

You don't need to figure out all of that today. In fact, you might not have it figured out by next weekend. What is more important is that you ask yourself this question frequently. This way, whenever a bright and shiny opportunity comes your way and will require good use of your time, you can ask yourself, "Do I really want this?" If not, then you move on. If so, then you take the bull by the horn and make the most of the situation. This way, you redesign yourself and improve on your ability to say no. Asking yourself this question frequently will offer your life a lot of clarity and direction.

- What is my identity?
  It will also help to redefine your identity. You would be surprised that many of the people the world refers to today as influencers, top leaders, and change agents never knew they would achieve the

kind of success they have achieved. They never also knew that their ideas would gain real traction. As a child, Van Gogh was told to stop making art by his mother. Michael Jordan was not accepted into the varsity team. Still, both knew what they wanted. Van Gogh wanted to pain, and Jordan wanted to play basketball. Where the tide of that passion would take them, no one knew. That's life. We don't know if you are the next big thing that will shape our world. In fact, you don't know it yourself!

I challenge you to take a look at any five great people or your choice. You will see that at least three of them did not find greatness by chance. Many of them already knew what they wanted and were working on it before they caught their big break. Jordan wanted to be an athlete. JK Rowling wanted to be published as a writer. Van Gogh wanted to create art. Steve Wozniak wanted to be the electrical guy. Serena Williams knew tennis was her passion and purpose. Usually, that is the story of most great men and women. Greatness and success hardly happen by coincidence or accident. It starts with identity. So, what is your identity? You don't need to sum up yourself in a sentence or word. You can start by being okay with who you are and who you aspire to be.

- Who can I serve?

   One of the time-tested secrets to getting what you want in life is service. Find what hurts the people around you and look for a way to solve it. In business, it is called a value proposition. You want to add value to the people around you. In your personal life, it is called being a decent human being. Every successful organization or business achieves success because of service. If you take service away, then a business cannot exist.

   Look at the people you love to be around—the people who light up your life and make you feel fulfilled. Ask them what hurts and what keeps them up at night. Ask them how you can be of help. If you make a practice of doing this (asking people how you can help), then you will see a lot of ways in which your life is valuable to others, and you will discover abundant opportunity to add value to others and yourself.

- Why not now?

As human beings, our brains like to take the path of least resistance. Our minds will want to push to the future any task that requires hard work or brain effort. It is human nature, and we have a word for it: procrastination. Instead of asking, "Why not now?", your brain wants to know why it can't be done tomorrow? One of the biggest ways to redesign your life is to take action on procrastination. If your brain is asking and giving you reasons why you should not do something now, I encourage you to write those reasons down. Afterward, stick the list somewhere on your desk where you can easily see and revisit it 30 minutes later. I can assure you that those few minutes of break can give you an amazing perspective and you will see that the reasons you wrote down on that paper are mainly silly. Actually, seeing them on paper can help disconnect from the chatter in your brain, proving to you that you don't need to wait until a time in the future when you can simply do it now.

Change is Good

6 Simple Ways to Live Your Best Life

Someone once said that the magic of life happens outside of our comfort zone. Yes, it may seem cliché, but there is nothing truer than that. Many women who like to cook often have an idea of what the perfect kitchen would look like. They know what color the wall tiles should be. They know the exact style of the oven they want. They know what type of fine china they want in the kitchen. But everyone knows that kitchens don't build themselves. You may need to search home brochures and look through the catalog of the local store where kitchen equipment is being sold. You probably need also to call a building contractor or interior designer. You will need to take time out of your schedule to take some difficult trips to design the kitchen you want. After that, you can keep making your magical recipes in your dream kitchen.

The same applies to our lives. You can't end up with the spouse of your dreams or accomplish your goals by being inactive. If we all feel successful, then there would be little incentive to be successful. If we already have everything we ever wanted in our lives, then would life be worth living? I don't think so. There would be nothing to strive for and nothing to gain from the struggle. So, why do anything in the first place?

Redefining Success

Every one of us has a worldview and perspective. We have what we are receptive to. We have our ideas and goals. We have personal experiences that constantly shape that worldview. Again, because we did not grow up in isolation, the worldview of others often rubs off on us. Because of this, the definition of success in life is varied. Success doesn't always mean more money, power, education, or influence—although many of us would like to have a good level of these in order to thrive in today's society.

You have to define what you want success to look like personally. It doesn't always have to be a grand idea or goal. Accomplishing little tasks that fit into the overall picture could be considered success. Perhaps getting published has always been a dream for you. In that case, finishing a chapter every week could be a success for you. For another person, it could be getting five new customers to walk into their store. What matters is that you have an end-goal in mind—a goal that makes sense to you. Success should not necessarily mean finding a "true path." It could be finding something that you're really good at—be it a calling, vocation, or dream—and then sharing that with the rest of the world in whatever ways you can.

Here's the thing: Success is not just some straight line or straight road on a long highway to happiness. Success is a bunch of zig-zags and curves, and while you may not take a straight shot towards success, you certainly can use those bends to your advantage and define how you want it to affect you.

To me, success means living a life you know you're capable of living and enjoying it while you're doing it. You may not feel successful. You may even feel you're stuck at the moment. But you always have the capacity to become unstuck and take the right steps forward in life. In that progress, you can feel very confident that you are doing something and taking whatever little steps you can to move forward towards your own success. It doesn't necessarily have to be hard to find a purpose in life—and maybe it's supposed to be so simple, too—but if you don't move towards some goals that you have created for yourself, then you'll for sure veer off the path before you get to your destination.

While you ponder on this, do remember you are driving the car you are in. You determine your own success in life, and nobody else. It may be hard to find or create your own path, but always remember that your failures do not have to define you. As a woman, you have the power to define your life—and no matter what anyone tells you, no one can ever take that away from you. You may land in a place you never expected and then flourish there. That doesn't mean that all the other experiences you have had in other places are worthless. Sometimes, we need to flounder before we find our success, and sometimes we can never find our purpose without experimenting a little bit.

Taking Action

The greatest courage in life is the courage to take responsibility for your own life. Whether you like it or not, you alone are responsible for the person you are today. Successful women develop a growth mindset, which means they are always in a state of constant and continuous improvement of self. They do not sit back and enjoy the skills and financial rewards they have accumulated up to this point. In fact, they are always curious to learn more, they are always striving to get better, they pay more attention to their health, they improve their soft and hard skills, and they acquire new skills that will set them on the path to success.

In order to redesign your life intellectually, you need to learn something new every day (although it may sound easier than it actually is). Still, it is possible. If you don't have the time to pick up a book or watch TV, you can certainly listen to podcasts in the car instead of listening to music all the time. That alone can help you gather a lot of knowledge, from dealing with the daily life stressors to starting up a new business venture or pitching investors. There are tons of podcasts on any topic that you can listen to. No one is implying that podcasts are the only solution here, but rather that knowledge is key. It is true that when you stop learning, you stop growing.

Design your life to include people who have the growth mindset. Your circle of friends is very important to your success in anything. If you want to be more fit and look healthier, you want to make friends with people who go to the gym frequently. Their passion will soon rub off on you. By spending time with them, you will experience and gain knowledge of techniques that will be useful to your health. If you want to start your own business, you will learn a lot more if you have an inner-circle of entrepreneurs. If you want to be a better researcher, you will learn faster if you insert yourself into a network of other researchers. The people who you allow into your inner-circle (family, friends, or partner) can all impact your mood, attitude, and your belief system—and even your strengths and weaknesses.

Work on your fears. One of the biggest obstacles to success is fear. Many of us could have been better students, better parents, and better leaders, but we are not because we are afraid of what people will think. We are afraid of going into a field dominated by men. We are afraid of what people will say if we start doing what we really want. We are scared of what the husband will say, yet we have not even tried. Sometimes, the things that scare us the most never happen. And what if they do happen? You are going to start a business, so what? You are not the first woman to do something unconventional. Or so what if you are the first? Fear is 'False Evidence Appearing Real.' The world would not go crazy if you did something that will give you fulfillment. If the world does go crazy, so be it. The world goes crazy now and then for something anyway. Challenge your fear and take action.

Avoid complacency. You can't just be comfortable with what you have and where you are. You need to strive for more. If you want to master your field, you need to devote more time to understanding the ins-and-outs of the field. Get out and meet people. Put in more time. Go to a new city. Expand your social circle, learn new opportunities, and refresh your enthusiasm by getting on new projects now and then.

Open your mind to opportunities. Allow people to talk and then listen to their side of the story. Hear out others' ideas. They key word is "hear," not "accept." You should only accept after perusing it and seeing that it fits into what you want for yourself. You need to have an open (not feeble) mind. On the path to success, you will come across people with a different worldview, sexual orientation, way of life, life philosophy, business principles, etc. You want to be open to people, but stay grounded in your belief and identity—the identity and belief that you have obtained by an understanding of who you are and where you are going.

Pat attention to money. At some point in our lives, we end up broke. We are short on money, jobs don't really pay us enough, and that brings on worry and stress.

However, what you need to remember is that in such times, stressing out won't do you any good. All it will do is waste more of your time—time you can channel into something productive. When I looked back to the days of my single life, I recognized I struggled to understand the importance of my financial well-being. It was filled with uneasiness when I contemplated when and where I spent my money. For instance, I never seemed to mind spending on lavish trips, even if it meant dipping into my emergency money. I wanted to travel, and that would overtake my thoughts of covering my expenses for emergencies. I often traveled (and lavishly, I might add). Then, a crisis hit my household. I lost my job due to the company going out of business. I thought, "My parents are going to flip when I tell them I need to move back home (as an adult with no savings)." To say the least, it was ugly. Fast-forward and I can now say it was the best lesson ever for me.

Financial wellness is a process in which you learn how to manage your finances and expenses successfully. It is true that in this day and age, we cannot do anything without money; it controls us. However, you should not let money be your driving force.

To promote your financial wellness, the first thing you need to do is differentiate between the things you want and the things you need. For example, you need food to eat and survive, but you don't necessarily need fast food to survive. Buying fresh groceries is cheaper than fast food. It is also a healthier option. Use public transportation instead of buying your own car. A car is not a need. Limit your spending on things like alcohol. We all know that it does more harm than good. Choose the safer and cheaper option. You'll be saving money as well as improving your health. Only spend your money on things you think are absolutely crucial. Save the rest for your future or your children.

For a good, solid foundation of financial wellness, you also need to start paying your bills on time. Delaying them will do you no good; it'll only worry you more. You'd come back home from work, switch on a light, and be reminded of the bills that are due. No one really wants to live a life under emotional torture and spend the rest of it stressing out, right? So, start paying your bills early and be free from debt!

When it comes to financial wellness and your relationship status, people tend to have mixed views. Some might consider improving financial wellness by being in a relationship, while others might think that financial wellness can only be achieved if you're single. While it is true that being in a relationship means your costs will be split between your boyfriend/girlfriend, being single also has its financial pros. For example, you get to decide what to do with your money and how you want to spend it. A single woman will be fine on her own financially, even if she's not in a relationship. It just requires a little bit of organizing and a clear, positive mind. You don't need to discuss everything with your partner first, either. Neither do you have to depend on them to pay the month's phone or electricity bill. Being single means: You can learn to survive on your own and be independent.

Eat right. You have the ability to put life back into your life and transform the way you look and feel by resolving to eat better and exercise, but it's easy for food to wield power over us and control us like a manipulative lover. Highly-addictive nonsense like processed foods and refined sugars make our receptors go haywire. Those devious chemicals pull the authority we have over our bodies from our fingertips. We start to go for a few butter-loaded cookies absentmindedly. We believe that just half of that donut at work won't hurt, but the now-dependent you conveniently forgets the many small slips you've had, and you fail to add up all the little here-and-there's.

As always, just one more delectable wedge of milk chocolate won't hurt.

You don't want to be dependent on food to merely survive—the kind of surviving that's fuzzy, coasting through life, feeling held under by your own self, and ultimately, withering away from missed opportunities. Rather, you want to use food to thrive and to form your body and mind into the best version of yourself. It's your moment to start taking back control of your life with healthy eating and exercise habits. There's never a better time to be your best self—not in a few days, next week, or on the first of next month. You deserve perfection now.

Mental and physical health begins inside. If you're ever going to unleash your inner and outer potential, you must nourish your mind, body, and spirit with vitality and sustenance. Say "I love myself" with a romantic, colorful dinner of surprisingly-filling roasted veggies. Skip drive-thrus full of fake foods and false hopes. Learn about and pay attention to labels. Make it seamless for yourself and step into a program that makes healthy living and eating simply.

Whenever I eat clean, I don't just feel better; I see better. It's like the dust is wiped from my vision and I remember what matters; why I'm on this earth and what my motivations are.

Working healthy eating habits back into your life is best married with soul-engaging, euphoric exercises. Lose your mind in Shavasana after a sweaty Vinyasa yoga class, and up your cardio to fill yourself with cleansing, restorative oxygen. Mixing a daily sweat into your life is intoxicating, and with each mile ran or stair climbed, your strength grows inside and out, and your dreams come closer to your reach.

Purposeful living starts with how you treat yourself. If you can remember just one thing, remember all that matters in life is your health. Your health can momentarily slip out of your hands—you just have to take it back. It takes 21 days to break bad habits. Go forward with the purpose and strength to exercise and eat right for a better you.

Start Today

6 Simple Ways to Live Your Best Life

There is no point waiting until tomorrow for what you can do today. You have the power to be remarkable. You have the power to change your wealth and health. You have the power to lose that weight. You have the power to eat right. You have the power to aspire to reach that top position in your organization. You have the power to lead that organization as a woman. Irrespective of how bad today might be or how far away those dreams may seem, it is never too late to create a better life for yourself and the people around you. Only you have the keys to your life, and only you can create your vision of success in the world. You only have to do what you think is best for you., and in that process of creating your own success, you will be successful. Just don't stop working. Refuse to be stagnant and refuse to secede the ownership of your life and vision to someone else or society.

Take baby steps if you want and then go from there. Little steps are better than no steps. If you want to publish a book, write a sentence now. Worry about grammar tomorrow. If you want to lose that weight, do that sit-up now. Don't look in the mirror; just do it. If you want to be an athlete, run around your block today. Don't wait until tomorrow. You build muscle slowly. That is the way you build success, too. You start small and then become big. Starting small makes you assume your identity, and by assuming your identity, you can take the first steps to become truly remarkable—but those baby steps matter the most!

Chapter Three

REIGNITING YOUR PASSION AND PURPOSE

There is a saying that goes, "Do what you want, and you will never work a day in your life." That is the first thing they tell you when you are about to start up your career. Seek passion first, and your work will never feel like 'work' because you will be so happy doing it! Now, this is true to a vast extent. In fact, if you are doing a job you are not passionate about in any way, you are bound to end up becoming miserable because every day, your life will lack light and enthusiasm. Every day, you will struggle to find happiness—something that's found only when you leave that job. The sad thing is that many of us feel this way daily. In my opinion, this happens for three major reasons:

1. You had the passion and have lost it.
2. You never had the passion at all.
3. You are experiencing burnout.

Many of us struggle a lot to understand what it is that we are truly passionate about and, quite unfortunately, you don't see a lot of passionate people in the workplace today. Even in our personal lives, discovering and following our passion are quite difficult things to do because of the way our society is structured and the demands that come with daily living. We would rather do a job that we hate but pays well now or do one that gives happiness or fulfillment but pays little. We would rather go to college and do a STEM course because of the financial prospect instead of attending a music school where our heart belongs. We would rather be a lawyer to avoid disappointing our parents instead of being a travel blogger. There are always things that push us away from what we are passionate about. Even if we are lucky to have found and pursued our passion, life throws us things that often sap up our passion and energy.

The very first step to reigniting your passion and purpose is to go back down memory lane and remember what you used to love. As we become grown up and attract more responsibilities, we tend to forget what we used to embed ourselves in as children. What were the things you used to love doing and could spend hours immersed in? For some, it could be watching football; for others, it could be being outdoors camping. For you, it could be playing a musical instrument, hanging out with people, helping someone at the local shelter, watching live musical performances, painting, etc. There is no end to these things. But I am sure that at least there was something you really loved doing that made you happiest a while ago. Maybe it was childhood. Perhaps it was something you found recently but haven't had the opportunity to engage more with it. Sit down and think about what used to make you happiest.

When you find that 'thing,' try to be more consistent with it. You owe it to yourself. Try to do it at least once a week. Perhaps it is dancing. Take a dance class at least once a week. Go to the gym. See how it makes you feel. See how you shift. Take the passion with you to the next day and see how you come alive and bring happiness to the lives of others. Perhaps you like to smile and laugh, but lately, you have judged yourself to be eccentric and have clammed up. Smile today. Brighten up your life.

Passion comes from within, and that is why sometimes it can be fleeting and elusive because instead of creating passion ourselves, we wait for the world to give it to us. We become passive and wait for passion and happiness to fall on our laps instead of putting ourselves in charge of the experiences we want to have. Unless you bring something to the table, no one will want to invite you to theirs. Therefore, by doing what you are passionate about constantly and consistently, you will train yourself on how to exercise your passion muscles.

Go outside of your comfort zone. Perhaps you can't really do the things you once loved because of injury or physical limitations. This doesn't mean you should give up on passion. What you need to do is start exploring. You will never know what activities may get your attention once you start engaging in them. In the end, it is up to you to generate the passion that will inspire you and others. When you become a master of that, you will start to experience an increase in your self-worth and net worth.

Like I mentioned earlier, sometimes the major reason for lack of passion could be just good old burnout from such things as daily tasks at work, dealing with family, or some other personal matters. In the workplace, burnout often happens when you feel like the work you are doing doesn't matter and you feel exhausted doing it. Why did you get into that job in the first place? Where do you want to go next? Look back to when you first started. What were you most excited about? What vision did you have for yourself at the time? Are you still running with that vision? If you are occupying some sort of leadership position, are you helping others reach their goals? Going back to the beginning can help you refocus your mind on why you started on that path. Most of the time, the recipe for curing burnout is taking a break. If possible, take a few days off from work, ask someone to watch over the children, delegate other duties to someone else, and just take a good break. Go to a good restaurant, have a delicious meal, visit the spa, get a massage, watch an orchestra performance—just do something that takes your mind off of work. Sometimes, we are often too buried in problems; we fail to see other perspectives. Taking a break can offer you a whole new perspective. It can give you fresh eyes so you can see things in a new light and reignite your passion.

Keep in touch with your community. The truth is that your job, like life, is a marathon. It is not a sprint. You will always have new tasks every day. You will always have children to handle every day. You will always have a business to run. You will always have meetings. If you want to sustain your passion, you need to have some pressure-release valves in your plans. This outlet for pressure should be your community. Keeping in touch with your community can really help you reignite your passion. Have deep conversations with like-minded individuals who are also passionate about the same things as you. These connections can help provide your mind with context and vision while helping you build a shared perspective. In the process, you may even create a sense of urgency as you start exploring new challenges in your work. You can reduce burnouts and find your purpose by staying in touch with people who live their mission and life's work on a daily basis. It will blow your mind how something like this can improve your motivation!

When you start experiencing burnout, disengagement, and a sense of purposelessness, you need to know that it is time to change things up. Take a break. Pause and connect. Evaluate your goals and values. Often, you will see that the tiredness you are experiencing is a result of the fact that your current goals do not align with your values, and you are pursuing a goal that doesn't align with your purpose.

Continue to learn. When was the last time you learned something new? In fact, a sure-fire way to keep fanning the embers of passion is to discover new things. Learning offers a window into understanding the world. It also beams light on new opportunities and improves your quality of life. The upside to learning is that you do not need to invest so much time in it to enjoy its benefits. Use the internet to see how best to manage tasks. It is important to schedule downtime in order to explore new ideas through reading, having deep conversations, attending classes or seminars, or simply observing others could help you gain new skills and insights.

It also helps to make a list of all your recent goals. Goals help you to remember that you aren't failing and that you have come a long way on this journey. Don't break down now! Listing all your recent accomplishments can help you to remember how far you have come since you started this journey as well as remembering the milestones that you have achieved in your career can open you up to reevaluating what you consider priorities. What aspect of your jobs do you love? Do you like mentoring your team? Do you like solving the problem of a challenging client? Do you love helping your team get better at solving their problems? The key is to remind yourself of what you used to love about your job in the first place. Understanding where you get the most satisfaction out of spending your time can get you energized and thinking more about how you can do more of the things that excite you.

As an appendage to the above, I would also advise that you get creative. Sometimes, the loss of passion can stem from doing things we already know how to do over and over again, to the point that we just don't feel excited doing it anymore because it is no longer challenging. But trying your hands periodically at something different can get you fired up. Creativity is a great motivator because it makes people very interested in what they are doing. It gives hope that an idea can actually be worthwhile while also giving the possibility that achievement is on the horizon. Creativity makes life more fun and more interesting.

We all have a unique ability to do something from our own perspective. Even if you don't think you're creative, you will see that it is just a matter of trying. You are capable of bringing life and captivating us all with your mind and thought process. Being creative can involve merely taking an idea and transforming it into another new form. It could be an article you found on the internet and then go about the task of modifying to reflect your feelings and thoughts. It could be a painting you saw that inspires a new form of hues and shapes in your head. I could be a new way to solve a technical problem or a new trick to get your co-workers to do something they don't want to do, all while thinking it is their own idea to do it. It could be an idea to have your children get their homework done on time. Many of the things that have become big things in life started out from a small, seemingly inconsequential idea. Facebook started out as an idea for some students to communicate at Harvard and then was put into "form." Today, the idea has grown into a platform for over a billion people throughout the world. It has also become a platform for information dissemination and a virtual goldmine for business owners. Sometimes, all you have to do is allow yourself to do! Allow yourself to create and then go from there. You may find passion in that thing! When you're not creating something, you're not allowing a part of your brain the ability to express you as an individual. Creating gives you a sense of purpose, builds excitement, develops a sense of ownership, and ignites your inner flame. So, think about it: What are you going to create today?

While you're thinking about that, you also want to contribute. A quote attributed to Howard Thurman says, "Don't ask yourself what the world needs; ask yourself what makes you come alive. And then, go and do that. Because what the world needs is people who have come alive." Nothing is truer than that.

Every action you take, every thought you act on, and everything you do affects someone else because we're all connected as a people, even if we are living thousands of miles away. So, what can you contribute to solving a problem? This is not about being the rescuer of souls, saint, or a Mother Theresa. It is simply about being your wonderful, fabulous, quirky self and showing up despite all your insecurities, fears, and limited beliefs in order to contribute to something larger than yourself. Being a contributor to a community can help raise your self-worth and help rekindle the fire of passion that you have always wanted.

Now that we are talking about community, it is important that you're constantly checking in with yourself and clearing out anything or anyone that's no longer serving you. Yes, it's time to cancel and delete any "stagnancies" in your life. Give yourself the respect to walk away from anything that is no longer serving you, growing you, or depleting your happiness.

When things feel static, energy gets trapped and doesn't flow with the natural rhythm of the universe—and that's the problem: You're stuck in a rut! Something needs to be taken away in order to create space for the new stuff. This can be anything from certain objects around your home or workspace, toxic people in your personal and professional life, self-limiting beliefs that have kept you as a prisoner in your mind for a long time, and things like societal expectations based on what you are "supposed to do as a woman" or "who you are supposed to be as a woman." Think about what you need to clear so that a wave of new energy has room to enter. Take inventory of the excess in your life and personal space. Clear out unnecessary items that no longer represent who you are in your current intention. This will help you stand in your "newness" and usher in the vibes of clarity and encouragement to keep you going.

Take a step back and assess your relationships, too. Whether it's your friend, girlfriend/boyfriend, parents, etc., assess how your relationship is with everyone. Holding onto the past does you no good. It is the past. There comes a time when you'll have to let it go, whether it was due to betrayal or failure. Once you let it go, you will feel free and be able to grow emotionally. Having more friends can mean having more special contacts, but these special contacts could be the cause of your downfall and tiredness. Less is often more. If you find there is any negativity in one of your relationships, don't hesitate to sever ties and move on.

Getting unstuck and more passionate is about making small, simple decisions and taking action. Always move away from what you don't want and towards what you do want. If you don't know what you want, then just continue to move away from what you don't want until you figure it all out. Life and living are all about the journey. When you follow your true worth and create new opportunities, you have different experiences and create for yourself the life you want. You can't just sit back and let things happen. That won't give you the quality life you want and deserve.

Chapter Four

REACTIVATING INNER CONFIDENCE

6 Simple Ways to Live Your Best Life

In my opinion, no one was born with low self-esteem. Self-confidence issues are issues we developed because of communal living. You develop low self-esteem because you measure your self-worth with others. You measure how beautiful you are by comparing yourself with Hannah. You measure how good your job is by comparing your job with Ava. You measure how good your children are by comparing them with your neighbor's. Your life doesn't seem to go well because Harry and Betty are so in love and seem happy every time, but you are still single. You seem miserable because your close friend has changed cars three times in the past two years, but you are still driving your old car from college. You can't wear the dress you want to because you don't know how your friends will see you. You can't spend money you have because you are concerned that your poor friends are going to think you are rubbing your good financial status in their faces. You don't want to ask that man to dinner because you are afraid of what he will think of you. You don't want to ask for a promotion to the position of supervisor or even ask for a supervisor's pay because you are afraid of what your boss will think, even though you are already doing the work anyway. I can go on and on, but I think you are starting to get the point: You need to give your confidence a kick.

Real inner confidence comes from really and truly believing you are worthy, just for being your wonderful self. It comes from not needing anyone's validation of the fact that you are awesome. As a woman, you believe in your abilities to reach for the sky, to lead, to be the best you can be, and to excel at career and family because you can. When you are confident in yourself, external factors do not matter. It was Dr. Seuss who said, "Today you are you. That is truer than true. There is no one alive who is You-er than you. Shout loud, 'I am lucky to be what I am!'"

Today, you want to quit attaching your value to things like your job, how much money you have or don't have in your bank account, how good you look, and other people's opinion of you. You want to focus on your unique traits and what makes you who you are.

Confidence is critical to excelling in life. Without it, most of us will never achieve success despite whatever strength or talent we have. There are tons of talented people out there who don't land the kind of deals they could have or start the kind of business they want because they simply do not have the talent. To put it simply: They are being held down by a lack of self-confidence

An important key to activating your inner confidence is watching your self-talk. Are you talking positively or negatively? What does your narrative sound like? If every time Oprah or Ellen walk to the stage and thought, "People said this and that about me in the tabloids yesterday. I'm not sure I can stand that camera today," do you think they would be able to affect lives positively like they have done today?

Picture this scenario: You live on the first floor of an apartment building. Your friend who just visited calls you to throw down the car key she forgot on your couch. The chances are you will likely make a good throw without overthinking it, and your friend will catch it with the most minimal effort. Now, imagine that you have to throw the same key the same distance, but with cameras watching and another 1,000 people watching as well to see if you fail and, if you do fail, you will lose $2 million. That changes things, right? You have the same set of skills in both scenarios, but the issue is that you stopped trusting yourself and second-guessed yourself, whereas if you just trusted yourself and threw the keys, you would find that

$2 million in your pocket rather quickly. Like Henry Ford said, "Whether you think you can or you think you can't—you're right."

Your inner voice doesn't always have to be your critic. It only becomes one when you let your negative experiences and feelings have an impact on it the most. You've probably heard the phrase 'Confidence comes from within.' There is a truth to that. It all depends on your mind and how you process what happens to you and everything around you.

I have to admit here that I have not always taken the time to listen to that small voice within me. You know the one...that voice that tells you not to do "that thing" or "don't go to that place."

If you find that you are kicking yourself down, realize that it's your fears speaking. Whenever one is afraid or feels vulnerable, negative thinking kicks in. It is how we protect ourselves from what we fear might be a difficult or dangerous situation. The problem is this: The mind of a person lacking confidence doesn't always see the distinction between an actual dangerous situation (a life-threatening one) and one that is simply imagined. Taking your career to the next level, asking that man out on a date, or performing with all your heart will not make you drop dead.

You also want to cut out the social comparison. You comparing your life to others will not take you anywhere. Comparisons don't really serve any purpose and are excuses you give yourself for being stuck where you are. If your mind starts to compare, ask yourself, "How will this help me? Will this move me closer to my goals or further away from them?"

You also need to know what you want. Having direction and clarity of mind and thought will help you move forward with confidence. Stephen Covey once said, "If the ladder is not leaning against the right wall, every step we take just gets us to the wrong place faster."

Realize that you will not be perfect. It's better to start dealing with that now. No one is. Don't beat yourself up for your shortcomings. Some of us chase after things just to show that we are right. We ponder on how to approach situations, conduct ourselves to the point that we get so filled with anxiety, and end up not taking any action at all or taking action in a way that shows a complete lack of self-confidence.

Learn to speak up for yourself, too. Open your mouth and say something about what you believe in. If you take a look at history, you will find that the people who have made a mark in this world are those who have spoken up when it matters, presented their ideas in the face of adversities, and have taken a chance on themselves. People remember Rosa Parks today because she stood up and spoke up when it mattered. No one is saying you should be a social activist, but at least be your own activist. Dare to say what you believe in. You will be surprised by who listens to you and is impressed by your confidence in sharing your ideas.

There will be people who doubt you, but that doesn't mean you should let that stop you from speaking up and taking a chance doing what you believe in. Criticism only means that you have people talking about you. People who have taken confident and bold steps have faced resistance. It is the way of the world. Stay focused on your belief and forge ahead.

Dress the part. How you dress goes a long way in order to make you feel confident. When you look good, you feel good. So, for an instant confidence boost, try these things: have a nice bath, choose something great to wear, put on some perfume, and do your hair. It is amazing the difference in doing these very simple things will have on your day!

Love yourself. Don't always look for validity and love from others. Give yourself the care that you'd expect from another and treat yourself gently. Indulge in a good book, take a walk, discover new music you can relate to, or take a day off and sleep in. All of these tiny steps help nurture you and make you confident.

Meditate. Meditation can really help you flush all negative thoughts from your mind. Focus on that one motivating phrase and welcome setbacks. Your setbacks and failures help you grow. They are lessons for you. In addition to that, meditation can help get rid of unnecessary stress and overthinking.

There is no guarantee that your loved one will stay with you forever. Always keep in mind that there may come or unhealthy. I reiterate: It is not your fault if they decide to stay small. That is their choice. Some haters will speak up and question your motives and declarations. Some may even call you names and make a lot of fuss about your personal life. Pay them no mind. Haters will try to sabotage your efforts, question your motivation, and smile in your face while whispering behind your back. But this is not about you. It is about your choice to make deliberate decisions, to stretch, to declare that you are good enough just as you are, and to own your amazing self. Those things will make them feel uncomfortable about themselves. Your haters are feeling threatened, scared, bewildered, or even self-righteous. In response, they lash out at you, all the while unsure of how to address the inconsistencies that abound in their own lives. That's not on you, honey; that's on them. You know what your job is? Ignore the haters. Feel empathy, pity, or amusement—but do not let them get to you. It's not your duty to please others; it's your duty and right to honor yourself in whatever way feels right and genuine.

Be accountable to self. If you are going to build your inner confidence, you will need to take accountability for your actions and reactions. When you stand up in your life and declare your intentions to live fully, love hard, lead responsibly, and honor your joy, you're also declaring your intention to take responsibility for the choices you make. It may not always feel this way every time, but the truth is that we always have the choice. We have a choice to wake up with a positive attitude every day. We have the choice to be generous with our love and share it with others. We have the choice to decide how we live our lives and what we stand for. We have the choice to follow through with our word. We have a choice in how we treat others. We have a choice in how we treat ourselves.

Truly realizing our ability to choose and honor our integrity helps us get freedom in our dreams, our actions, and our quest to live our lives intentionally. Let your words and actions have weight. The effort is very well worth the self-respect it creates.

Allow others to be amazing. When you are confident in your own gifts and ways of expressing yourself, only then can you celebrate the awesomeness of the people around you without feeling you lack in some way. You can encourage your competitor! You can celebrate the success of your co-workers without feeling threatened! You can genuinely admire the brilliant ideas of other women without feeling jealous! You can appreciate the intelligence of your siblings without feeling like you have to make a point!

The converse of this is true, too. When you celebrate the awesomeness of others, you are sending little grenades of inspiration to your psyche. When you appreciate someone's creativity, intelligence, compassion, love, or productivity, you'll discover compassion, intelligence, creativity, and productivity in your own life.

You attract what you like and celebrate. What you notice and celebrate in others will come up more often in your own life, too. Let your belief be built in abundance and the power of support by truly treasuring the amazing people in your life.

Sharing is caring. Share your gift with the world. Use your talents to give back to the people in your community. Start a side gig. Start a side hustle that allows you to show your strengths to the people who need them. Help out and give generously with your time, energy, and talent. Don't be concerned about yourself for one minute. Share your gift. By doing so, you are confirming that you indeed have something worthwhile to contribute, that you make a lot of difference, and that your presence is appreciated—all of which are good for building your inner confidence.

Putting yourself out there by helping someone, volunteering for a cause you care about, teaching a child how to do something you love, or starting a business is good for you and everyone in the world. So, you see? It's a win-win!

Having a bad perception of yourself won't help you in any way. Nothing is stopping you, except a small, nagging voice that says you're not enough. Ignore it! Now is your time to shine and soar high!

Chapter Five

RETHINKING YOUR SUCCESS NETWORK

In the second season of the very commercially-successful Netflix comedy series, *Orange is the New Black,* viewers were introduced to a flashback scene between Red, a Russian inmate who is in control of the prison's kitchen, and Vee, an African-American inmate who is in control of the illegal heroin distribution in prison. Both are leaders of their respective groups.

In the flashback, Red was a newbie at prison life and very scared of prison activities. Vee, on the other hand, was a crime veteran who understood power and relationship dynamics, especially as it applies to dealing with fellow criminals. Being roommates, Vee extended a hand of friendship to Red and they became friends. Not too long after that, Red identified a business opportunity in prison by virtue of her position as the leader of the kitchen workgroup. Through the weekly delivery of supplies to the kitchen, she was now able to smuggle things in that other inmates needed. In prison, the ability to provide contraband (such as cigarettes) offers a lot of negotiating power. Soon, Red begins to be the go-to person for things that inmates couldn't get on their own. She began to amass power and people did her bidding because she would punish anyone who crossed her path by way of to pay attention to. Therefore, you would rather pay attention to things you can see—things that are superficial and things that other people consider important.

What is ironical is that your success is very well dependent on the quality of the relationship you have and the experience you are able to get. It's like the popular saying, "It is not what you know, but who you know." While no one is trying to make an excuse for nepotism, this statement is very true to a very good extent. Whenever an opportunity shows up in our workplace or another organization that we know about, the first person who comes to your mind is that friend you care about, even if she is not the best graduate of the class. You remember her because she is your friend and you can vouch for her. Then, you make a recommendation. You don't remember some guy you read about in the newspaper who graduated at the top of his class from Harvard. That is simply the way life works. In fact, for many high-level positions in many organizations, recruitment is usually made from the recommendations of management-level staff. This is also true for some entry-level positions. It is not unusual for organizations to tell the staff to look into their network and recommend candidates for vacant positions. Ideally, it's better to hire someone your staff can vouch for than another person they don't know much about. People want to offer opportunities to those they know, people they have shared and build life experiences with, people they can trust, and people who make them happy. This is why, for any stage of your life—whether you are chasing some personal or professional goals—relationships are important. As a leader, relationships are important. As a follower, relationships are important.

If today was your last day on earth, what would you regret the most? To make it easy to answer this question, let's make some options available. Will you wish you had:

1. Acquired more degrees and certifications that would have led to rapid career growth?
2. Invested more money in Apple, Google, Amazon, and Microsoft?
3. Spent more time with the people you care about?

Chances are you are thinking about the third option because when it comes to our last moments, the first two don't matter. So, can we assume that we all know what is right? Yes, we can. But for some reason, we don't always do the right thing. We know that having good relationships with the people around us is good, but we rarely make it an important priority until it is too late.

Rethinking Relationships

The first step to redefining success is reevaluating the value of relationships. A study by Harvard called "The Grant Study," conducted between 1939 and 1944, sought to understand what made people happy and healthy. The study found that lasting and positive relationships with the people who surround us and the people we love and respect are the key. The study, which was a lengthy one carried out by generations after generations of researchers who observed the lives of 724 people born in Boston, talked to their families, asked questions about their health and family, and discussed how their lives have evolved over time. They found that those who had positive relationships with the people in their lives lived longer, experienced personal happiness, and enjoyed sound health—considerably more than those who didn't.

Having positive relationships with others based on trust, respect, and love increases our lifespan and makes us happier. With the knowledge that we can count on the people around us, even if they do not agree with us more than half of the time, gives a feeling of security. Most of us will spend at least 40 hours every week with other people, so we might as well decide to enjoy our relationships with them.

It is important to note that no matter how brilliant your mind or strategy is, you can't win against a team. That is why athletes need coaches, actors need directors, students need teachers, doctors need nurses, politicians need campaign managers, and children need parents. The list is endless! Everywhere you go, you will find tons and tons of examples where working as a team has trumped individual efforts because the truth is that you can't really do it alone. If you think that all you have become today is a result of only your effort, then you have not really been thinking deeply. Every single person who pointed you in the way you should go, every person who gave you advice, every person who facilitated access in one way or the other so you can achieve your goal—whether big or small—are all part of your success story. You can't live in total isolation. No one does. In the workplace, relationships are of high importance, too. If you want to accelerate your career and achieve your goals quickly, you will need the help and support of other people. You will need to surround yourself with a team of allies and advisors with whom you grow over time.

Creating an Inner Circle

If you look at the most successful people in the world today, you will find that many of them have one another on speed dial. The elites know the importance of an inner circle. That is why many of them buy apartments and school their children in areas where there are high net-worth individuals like them. People open doors for those they know and trust. Building strong relationships with co-workers, clients, and vendors are all equally important for creating long-term professional success.

When you surround yourself with an inner circle of powerful and successful people with mindsets such as yours, they can help you work on your weakness. Some of these people would have walked the same path you are walking and can help protect you from possible pitfalls on the way. These people don't necessarily have to be popular figures; they could even be people who are on the same journey with you. They don't have to famous or popular. They just have to be people who have the capacity to change your life for the better through their experience, perspective, encouragement, and guidance. Perhaps you want to start your own company that will create a meaningful product or offers a service that will solve a pressing issue while staying profitable, then you will need to have an inner circle of people who have done the same. You may need to attend industry events such as networking events and conferences to meet these people. You may need to reach out through emails and phone calls to request meetings.

As you are doing all of this, you should also be uprooting and weeding out the people you don't need in your life. Don't keep negative people around you who won't value your drive to excel. You don't want to be around people who will not add value to you. They only want you to fulfill their needs.

Your network should include people who can innovate, think, listen, advise, encourage, hold you to a higher standard, and, more importantly, reprimand you when you don't do the right thing. As you are looking out for people like this, make sure you also listen. Your eyes and ears should be on high alert.

So, how can this be done?

6 Simple Ways to Live Your Best Life

The first step is to perform a personal assessment of yourself. Are you in control of your life right now or is it being controlled by other people? When was the last time you made a conscious effort to reach out and meet people because of the value they can provide to your goals? Do you always come off as desperate? Do you show potential and insight in your communication? Do you make them happy spending time with you? The truth is people most often want to get value for their time, too. Although relationships should not be transactional, a mutually-beneficial relationship is always nice to have. You also need to be on the lookout for how to help others—not because you expect people to help you in return, but because being useful and generous is a good way to build social capital as people don't forget those who show up for them in times of need. It communicates that you are valuable and useful.

Secondly, you need to assess your habits and activities. What kind of activities did you participate in within the past two weeks? Was it worth your time? Where would you rather invest your time and effort? What would you stop doing totally? Are you spending your time in a way that aligns with your values and goals? If it is not, this is the time to backtrack.

Thirdly, you want to assess others. Look at the three people you spend the most time with. Do their lives reflect the goals you want to achieve? It is not a myth that you are the average of the people you spend the most time with. The idea is not to cut off ties with friends simply because they do not reflect your goals. Instead, seek out the people who do and spend more time with those people.

Shrinking your inner circle gives you the opportunity to create your own environment. As you begin to move deeper, you start to create more authentic relationships with a small number of people who are truly important to you. You will start to gain perspective into their needs and they, in turn, will also develop a bigger understanding of you, thus giving you a stronger platform upon which you can build a bigger community that benefits from knowing you and your inner circle. You don't need a giant-sized network.

The kind of people you want to have in your network will depend on your professional goals. This is why the first point about doing a personal assessment is critical. But if you are still unsure about where to start, it doesn't hurt to look at a few suggestions. The following are some traits that may be very valuable for you to consider:

- Trusted Confidant

    During an adventure, whether in your personal or professional life, you may need someone to listen to your plans and assess them. You want someone who is unbiased and understands secrecy and discretion about all the things you have discussed. This person will be well-rounded, have knowledge about a variety of subject matters, and able to give you advice that is holistic, supportive, and constructively-critical. You need to exercise caution when picking your confidant since they will be a custodian of your thoughts, strategies, and fears.

- Confident Traveler

    There is always some benefit to having in one's network someone who has a good appetite for risk-taking and highly-inquisitive mind. Usually, this person would be an excellent conversationalist with immense knowledge of culture and a wide network of people. They will usually have the contact information of almost everyone they have met and are very resourceful. They would probably tell you they key person you need access to at a beach party or honky-tonk. The confident traveler has a wide perspective of the global market and culture and can help give advice about the possibilities of moving into a space that is not your comfort zone. If you are trying to move into an international market, this is the person you would want to bounce your ideas off of. The interesting thing is that they would most likely also want to jump on board with you since it gives them an opportunity to experience a new adventure!

- Inspiration Fountain

    This is someone you definitely want to have in your network, irrespective of whatever your goals are. Why? Because plans become a mess the moment you start executing them, and you will need someone to stay with you and fire your motivation when this mess happens. And messes do happen—not because your plan is not solid but because there are often too many variables in a career plan that you may not be able to predict. This person may have a direct influence on your leadership qualities, helping to build your confidence and challenging you in ways you never thought possible. Typically, this person may serve as a mentor, as they are usually very successful in their business endeavor. Therefore, you want to be prepared whenever you are with this person because they never slow down for you to catch up with them.

- Financial Genius

    Money is important. Very important. And it doesn't matter whether you are working for a firm or own your business. You need to have people in your network who have a working knowledge of money metrics. This person would definitely have years of experience working in the finance industry or worked in some top-level finance position in a respectable firm. The bonus of having this person in your circle is being able to consult them on your professional financial goals or investments, and you can embrace their advice and information on organizations that are making impressive gains in the local and international markets.

- Social Butterfly

  Your social behavior affects your relationship. It defines who you are attracted to and who is attracted to you. In fact, to a large extent, it defines the extent to which you will be able to network. Usually, people who are funny and charismatic tend to have the most friends and know the most people. You probably went to school or work with one already. They know how to walk into a room and light it up. Often, they are the life of the office party. They often know someone who knows another someone who works somewhere else. Having this kind of person in your network can help build your own charisma and confidence. Even if this person doesn't rub shoulders with prominent people, their ability to easily warm themselves up to people can teach you a thing or two about how to interact with people who may seem unapproachable. It may also teach you about communication and social interactions, which is very helpful at industry events and everyday relationships with co-workers.

  Irrespective of whosoever you have decided to add to your inner circle, always make sure they are on your team and truly want to see you succeed. There will be challenges. As they come, we all want to be alongside someone who has our best interests at heart and will demonstrate genuine loyalty to our cause.

- Maintaining Your Network for the Long-Term
Now that we have talked about the importance of building an inner circle, it is also imperative to figure out how to maintain such a close network over time. How exactly do you maintain this network so that whenever you need help, you can easily reach out? Also, how frequently should you keep in touch with your inner circle? How do you balance bringing new people into the fold while still maintaining communication with those you have known for a while? If you are not staying in touch with your inner circle, then you will be losing out on a lot of potential opportunities.

One of the key things you can do to maintain your inner circle is determine the people in your network you want to consider a priority. It might be beneficial to put these people into subcategories. For example, the people in your network could be grouped into current clients, powerful colleagues, and friends who are high connectors. You then try to figure out, based on our needs and goals, how you want to allocate your attention. There may be others in the group you just keep in touch with for no serious reason except that they have a pleasurable company that you enjoy. It is probably best to think about how your relationships impact you. Do you feel happy after ending a phone conversation with that person? Do your problems get solved after talking to this person? If you are happier or closer to your goal after talking or meeting with this person, then you should try to keep in touch with them regularly.

The world is now a global village. Wherever you are, you can still keep in touch with all the available communication tools that are readily available. Send emails, use social media apps, request a coffee date, send a handwritten note, or place a call. The choice is really up to you. What tool you want to use in nurturing the relationship is up to you. The key to maintaining your inner circle is to be within their range, and that does not necessarily refer to the physical. What it means is that you have to keep in touch constantly so that it ensures you are still on top of their minds. One good way to do this is to take steps that show you care about the person and are interested in them. Be aware of when news or other information triggers you to think of that person. Perhaps you found something they have always wanted or discussed a subject they are crazy about with another person. Maybe you met a mutual connection. Those are usually good opportunities to keep in touch. Good relationships require nurturing to blossom. If you care enough about the person being in your network, then you should not only contact this person in your moment of need.

It also helps to use social media strategically. You can easily stay connected to people as long as they live through social media. But there is a caveat: Over-reliance on social media as a way of maintaining relationships with your inner circle can be harmful. In much the same way a phone call is not better than a face-to-face message, there is a different level of fidelity built into social media. Social media makes us feel like we have a strong connection with someone when, in fact, the relationship doesn't go beyond social media. That notwithstanding, you should use social media to your advantage. You can send direct messages and retweet content on Twitter, and share their posts on Facebook. It helps the most to have the conversation taken offline. If, for instance, you got information that the person was promoted, it then pays to send them a note, give them a phone call, or send a card with a congratulatory message.

The point of having an inner circle is for everyone to be an asset to one another. You can sustain a good relationship with people by looking for ways to be of help. You should listen very carefully to the challenges they have and help them sort it out (if you are able). Perhaps you have a friend whose younger sister needs a place to intern. It doesn't hurt to talk to your manager or other people in your professional network, like clients and co-workers, to see if they know about any internship openings. Or maybe a coworker needs help planning for an event. It won't hurt to let them know you have a grill, truck, or other things you feel they might need. It might even be people. Offer to help, but make sure that your motives are pure. It is good to help others, but doing so to get favor only shows that you want to impress them—which no one appreciates. You don't want to lose their respect and make them feel like you are kissing up to them.

Maintain humility. While it is good for people in your network to know about your professional success, you want to be careful about the way you communicate this success so as not to appear like a braggart. Instead, simply inform your inner circle about what you have been up to and provide them with the information they do not have about you. It can be much more helpful. You don't need to roll out the drums and start a personal brand promotion campaign. Instead, keep in touch and keep their memories of you alive.

Now, being friends with someone is not by force. If you have tried multiple times to keep in touch with someone and that person doesn't appear like they have the same desire as you to stay connected, it is probably a good idea to let them be. Don't burden yourself with the stress of a relationship where connections are not mutual because just as it is with any relationship, no one likes a desperate and needy person. Don't force a connection that is not there.

6 Simple Ways to Live Your Best Life

Be thankful. You didn't get to where you are in isolation. If you can, pause and try to flash back to the life-changing decisions you have made that got you to where you are now regarding your career. One or more of them are probably due to the advice someone gave or something someone said in passing that made you think twice about the path you are on at the time. All our lives, some of us have had parents, siblings, co-workers, bosses, mentors, teammates, church leaders, etc., who try to put us on a certain path that they believe will lead to the life and career that will give us satisfaction.

These people deserve recognition and appreciation. That person who encouraged you to apply for that job when you felt that you didn't meet the requirements deserves a thank you. Your friend who offered their shoulders for support when you were trying to get a job and kept getting disappointed deserves a phone call of appreciation. Your mentor who advised about changing career paths into the more rewarding one that you are working right now deserves an appreciation email. Team members who took the time to review your projects and proposals numerous times and offered feedback before you delivered it to the board deserve a thank you speech.

Your significant other who was always there to pick you up after a sad, long day at work and keeps encouraging you when you think you can no longer walk through the doors deserves some praise. The friends and relatives who have recommended you for jobs, scholarships, and projects that have all contributed to what you are professionally deserve a thank you. Friends who reviewed your resume and helped you prepare for that interview deserve a thank you note. If you are capable of introspection, you will find that you can't thank people enough. And even though there are far too many people to thank, you will still be on the right track if you practice appreciation one person at a time.

Many of us forget the people who were there for us when we get the job. We suddenly become too busy to make time for those people who took their time to lend their support. We do not respond to their calls, emails, and texts. Over time, we tend to lose contact with them totally, or we only reach out when we need something like a reference or connection to a company that we are very much interested in. Take some time out today to reach out and say thank you to those people. Take a moment to reach out and connect to them in a real and genuine way.

Therefore, never forget those who helped you get to where you are today. From experience, there are many people—personally and professionally—who have helped to shape my career and reputations as a leader. Sometimes, even the smallest bits of advice (which may not be recognized at the time) can have a long-lasting impact. Recognize those who helped you and keep them in your inner circle. It is always great to repay the debt.

Audit your group from time to time. You can decide to look at a list of your contacts and ask yourself if the list is still relevant. Think about it. Who should you add to the list? Who is no longer relevant? With time, your list will be recycled. This does not mean you will not talk to those people; it only means it may not be as often as you used to. Bringing new people into the fold and staying in touch with your old contacts should not be something you will be trying very hard to balance. Instead, try to mix old and new people when you can. This can give you the opportunity to learn and grow.

Chapter Six

READY? SET! RELEASE!
GEARING TO BE SUCCESSFUL

You might have heard the saying, "If you fail to plan, then you plan to fail." It might be overused, but that does not make it less accurate.

The road to success, whatever it is for you, is a marathon and not a sprint. You will need to condition your mind and change your mindset and actions to properly align in order to get you to the finish line. But before you get to the finish line, you will need markers. These markers are what will guide you so that you don't run off the track.

Ready (Assess Yourself)

First and foremost, you have to be honest with yourself. Understand that nobody is keeping a score with you; you are only competing with yourself. Therefore, take all the time you need to look deep and inward about your life. Some questions you might need to ask yourself include:

- Where am I now?
- Where do I want to be?
- How fast do I want to get there?
- What am I willing to give up?
- What do I need to close the gap between where I am and where I want to be?

with people? Am I hospitable to and able to welcome people?

What comes naturally to you?

You might think that everyone is excellent at the same thing you are, which is why it is not a skill for you—but you are wrong! There is no one like you.

Can you pack a car with luggage better than anyone? Can you beat anyone in Cosby Show trivia? Do you love to talk on the phone? Nothing is off-limits here. Just start writing and do not stop. Now, start looking for patterns.

Start by grouping your lists. The following are ideas:

- Things I love doing
- Things I get paid for
- Things I get paid the most for
- Things I want to improve on
- Things I haven't done in a long time

The point of looking for patterns is simply for you to see that you are good at many things and that you are better or even GREAT at a few specific things.

Whether you have all of the list completed or not, I now want you to go to five people who know and love you. Ask their opinions on what they see and value in you.

Set (Make a Plan Based on Your Assessment)

Now that you know where you are, it is time to dive deep into where you want to go. It is time to dream. We all have dreams…at least I hope you do. How boring of a life would it be if you never dreamed? Having a dream is great! You need to dream, and you need to dream BIG. When I say 'big,' I mean really get that head of yours up in the clouds type of dream! If you can't dream big, then you are going to aim small—and you'll accomplish even smaller.

But Break Down the Dream

Once you've stretched and risked in the dreaming stage, be sure to come back down to earth. Most people fail at this critical step. Breaking down that gigantic pie-in-the-sky dream into smaller bite-sized pieces of pie can be a daunting task.

And this is how the break down goes…

- Dreams are broken down into Visions.
- Visions are broken down into Mission Statements.
- Mission Statements are broken down into Goals.
- Goals are broken down into Action Steps.

Dreams are the grandest manifestation of what you hope and desire. It's hard to put your finger on it and usually lacks detail. But when you lose yourself in thought about your wants in life, your mind and imagination wander toward your dreams. Typically vague, ethereal, and possible, dreams are difficult to attain at this high level.

Own your dream. Don't let the dreams of others scare or intimidate you. Comparison is the thief of joy. You cannot make progress until you embrace the process. So, embrace your dream! Don't run anyone else's race. Go with your own idea. Dream your dream. Dream BIG!

Then, Create Your Vision

Having vision is a bit difficult to teach, but a Vision Board can make it a lot easier. If you are finding it hard to have a vision, then a Vision Board might be of immense help. A Vision Board is a physical image of what you dream—

the possibility of your dream moving from your mind into real life. This doesn't have to look like a ransom note with magazine cut-outs. You can use real pictures, quotes, inspiring art, etc. that represent your dream.

What does it feel like to accomplish that dream? Put it all on your board and put your Vision Board somewhere where you will see it every day.

In creating your vision, it might really help to create a good Mission Statement because:

> *"Without a really good Mission Statement, you have the potential to get to the top of the ladder only to find it leaning against the wrong building. The Mission Statement is further clarification and definition for your dreams and vision and assures you that your goals are aimed at the right target."*
> ~ Dave Ramsey, EntreLeadership ~

You also need to set goals. With goals, you can take actionable and timely steps towards your vision. Goals are the same as visions and dreams, except they are specific and well-defined in an order that you can actually attain them. The best way to set a goal is to set

SMART Goals:

SPECIFIC
MEASURABLE
ATTAINABLE
REALISTIC
TIMELY

Many excellent productivity books go over SMART Goals. A quick Google search will give you a lifetime to read up on. For your SMART Goals to work, they have to be yours. How can you make your dreams tangible if your goals are for someone else's dream?

Release (Execute)

One last leg of this process is when the going gets tough, and the lazy lose out. Putting feet to your goals-in-action steps is almost too simple to write out. So, most people don't. Most people do not want to do the work to accomplish the things they say they so desire. As such, most don't get to the action steps. Don't be "most people."

On taking action, you just have to do it. I can preach, teach, persuade, and even beg you all I want, but if you are not ready to take action, none of those things will work. Therefore, you have to decide on what you want and go for it. This is one thing no one can do for you. Your spouse can help you plan your financials, but they can't go to work with the mindset of making money for you. You have to take the steps. Will you fall? Probably! Maybe even twice or thrice. But you will be alright in the end.

Look at your Vision Board. Is your plan to have a big ranch of about 10 acres or more? Great! Go out and look for that ideal land. Talk to real estate agents or landowners. Get the quotes for different lands based on your needs. Compare the cost to know the average price you will need to work towards in purchasing the land. Figure out a way to raise the money and so on. Actions are important to achieve anything. They are equally as important as assessment and planning. So, think outside the box. Take the actions you have written down and one-by-one, try to achieve them one step after the other. Truthfully, it may not be easy. However, in the end, it will pay off.

We can dream, have Vision Boards, and make lists all we want. But until we put our foot to the ground and execute the plans, we aren't actually doing anything. You've

6 Simple Ways to Live Your Best Life

Over the years, Cai, experienced broken relationships, the loss of loved ones, serious illness among many life situations and found that the depth and breadth of the lessons learned were similar to those she coached. She created a system to help others through the singleness process. Prior to in a book, Coach Cai, empowered women in groups and workshops. Her vision is to offer women simple solutions in chaotic times to assist them in releasing their best lives, through forming a community, building networks and providing them related resources.